**W9-BNT-733**

# Wilma Rudolph

# Wilma Rudolph

## Athlete and Educator

### ALICE K. FLANAGAN

**Ferguson Publishing Company**
**Chicago, Illinois**

Photographs ©: AP/Wideworld: 14, 17, 23, 31, 36, 38, 41, 44, 48, 50, 52, 57, 61, 62, 65, 68, 69, 71, 72, 77, 79, 96, 98; Archive Photos: cover, 8, 58, 64; Corbis: 82, 84, 87, 88, 94; Liaison Agency: 92.

An Editorial Directions, Inc. Book

Library of Congress Cataloging-in-Publication Data
Flanagan, Alice K.
    Wilma Rudolph, athlete and educator / by Alice Flanagan.
    p. cm.—(Ferguson's career biographies)
    Includes bibliographical references and index.
    ISBN 0-89434-356-4
    1. Rudolph, Wilma, 1940–1994—Juvenile literature. 2. Runners (Sports)—United States—Biography—Juvenile literature. 3. Women runners—United States—Biography—Juvenile literature. [1. Rudolph, Wilma, 1940–1994. 2. Track and field athletes. 3. Afro-Americans—Biography. 4. Women—Biography.] I. Title. II. Series.
GV1061.15.R83 F42 2000
796.42'092—dc21
[B]                                                                                    00-037624

Copyright © 2000 by Ferguson Publishing Company
Published and distributed by
Ferguson Publishing Company
200 West Jackson Boulevard, Suite 700
Chicago, Illinois 60606
www.fergpubco.com

Printed in the United States of America
X-8

# CONTENTS

# INTRODUCTION

O LYMPIC RUNNER Wilma Rudolph was called the fastest woman in the world. At the 1960 Summer Olympics in Rome, Italy, she became the first American woman to win three gold medals at the same Olympics. But Wilma Rudolph began life with a less-than-promising start. When she was only six years old, doctors said that she would never walk without the aid of braces. Her determination to be normal and accepted by her peers proved every doctor wrong.

Wilma Rudolph's story is an example of

*Wilma Rudolph won three gold medals at the 1960 Summer Olympic Games in Rome.*

courage and perseverance, discipline, and hard work. It is the stuff champions are made of. It is the legacy heroes leave to their followers. Wilma Rudolph's life as a champion and a hero holds an important message for us all: "With a positive attitude, determination, courage, and hard work, there is little we cannot do."

# OUT OF POVERTY AND PAIN

WILMA GLODEAN RUDOLPH was born on June 23, 1940, in Clarksville, Tennessee. She was the twentieth of twenty-two children born to the Rudolph family. Born prematurely, Wilma weighed only 4 1/2 pounds (2 kilograms) at birth. For the next ten years of her life, she struggled to survive one illness after another. She was bothered by frequent colds and childhood illnesses such as measles and chicken pox. A serious bout with double pneumonia followed by scarlet fever left her thin and very weak.

## Polio and Paralysis

Then, when she was about five years old, Wilma was stricken with polio, a viral disease. Polio damages nerve cells of the brain and spinal chord. The devastating illness left Wilma's left leg partially paralyzed. Doctors said that she would never walk without a leg brace. They fitted her with a steel brace, which clamped onto her leg just above the knee and went down to her shoe. The heavy brace was supposed to help keep her leg straight. Wilma wore the brace from the time she got up in the morning until she went to bed at night. To help her walk better, Wilma also wore heavy brown shoes.

The brace and the shoes helped Wilma get around but did little to improve her feelings about herself or her relationship with other children. During most of her childhood, Wilma desperately tried to be normal and growing up poor in a family of twenty-two children didn't help. Being disabled caused most of her attempts to fail. But with the aid of a loving family and her own strong character, Wilma eventually overcame these obstacles. Her success in sports made her peers stand up and take notice of her. With "true grit," Wilma turned her disabilities into remarkable abilities that set her apart from others.

Wilma learned much about true grit from her parents. Both of them worked at several jobs to provide for their children. Although they never made more than $2,500 a year, Ed and Blanche Rudolph didn't take handouts from anybody. They even refused to accept welfare assistance from the government.

Wilma's father worked as a porter for the railroad and did odd jobs around town to add to his income. He painted houses, cut firewood, and worked as a handyman. Wilma's mother cleaned houses for wealthy white families and sometimes cooked in the local white café. At home, she ran the household and cared for her husband and children. Late at night, like many poor mothers, she sewed dresses and shirts for the children out of cotton flour sacks. In those days, flour sometimes came in sacks made from pretty cotton prints. With so many children to feed and care for, it was never easy making ends meet. The Rudolphs made do with what they had and taught their children to do the same. Looking back on this time of her life, Wilma said, "We did not have too much money back then, but we had everything else, especially love."

*When Rudolph was growing up, African-Americans and Caucasians seemed to live in two different worlds.*

## Inequity in the South

Wilma learned early about the inequalities that existed between blacks and whites in the South. She said, "I was four or five when I first realized that there were a lot of white people in this world, and that they belonged to a world that was nothing at all like the world we black people lived in." In those days, there were separate drinking fountains and restrooms for blacks and whites and separate sections in buses and restaurants. Blacks could not buy things on credit and were denied opportunities for jobs and education.

Wilma often resented the fact that white people had so many modern conveniences in their homes and yet they hired people like her mother to clean their houses and serve them breakfast in bed. "The way my mother worked," Wilma said, "somebody should have been serving her coffee in bed on Saturday mornings. Instead, she did the serving."

Many black children in the South were raised to accept life as it was. Wilma wrote in her autobiography: "A lot of black kids were raised that way down South, accepting things that weren't right. . . . The parents thought they were protecting the children . . . from trouble or from pain. If you accepted it, didn't rebel against it, things would be easier for you, they figured."

Religion helped many black people deal with these inequalities. Having faith and hope strengthened them and kept them from becoming bitter. The Rudolph family was very religious. Wilma's mother and father were strict Baptists. Her father was the disciplinarian in the family and ruled with an iron hand. Wilma wrote: "When my father got home, everybody got quiet. He laid down laws like, 'No church on Sunday mornings, no nothing else.' He took a lot of pride in the fact that he had twenty-two kids, and not a single one of them was ever arrested for a crime, or picked up by the police for anything, or ever went to jail."

Wilma said that her father believed education was the most important thing in life. He expected Wilma and her siblings to work hard and behave at school. He always told his children: "If you get a whipping at school, the first thing you can expect when you get home is another one." He demanded that his children show respect for all adults, no matter who they were. If he heard that one of his children disobeyed an adult, he punished the child.

*Young Wilma (right) with her older sister Yvonne. The future track star was six years old.*

## Beginning School at Home

Wilma was six years old before she realized that she was different from other children. Because of her disability, Wilma could not join in their games. When she tried to play with them, some children called her a "cripple." Wilma's brothers and sisters tried to protect her from the teasing, but they could not always prevent it.

At the age of six, most children were attending school. Because of Wilma's condition, she could not go to school. Instead, a teacher came three times a week to Wilma's home to bring her schoolwork. Wilma often recalled those times. "I sat around the house a lot," she said, "while the other kids my age were in school. There really wasn't much to do but dream. I would tell myself, 'I don't know yet what the escape is going to be, but Wilma, it's not going to be like this forever.'" Wilma's curious nature made her wonder about the world outside Clarksville, Tennessee. Even at that early age, she daydreamed about adventures elsewhere.

Because Wilma's family had no health insurance, her mother used home remedies to care for her. She made mixtures to rub on Wilma's leg, but they did little to improve her condition. When Wilma was six, her mother began taking her to the Meharry Hospital in Nashville, a hospital for black people founded by two black doctors. Wilma went there twice a week for four years to get massages and whirlpool treatments. The four-hour treatments were painful. For the first few years, Wilma's mother or aunt took her on the Greyhound bus to the hospital in Nashville. It took about an hour to make the 50-mile (80-kilometer) journey. The long bus ride gave Wilma a chance to get out of Clarksville. It opened up a new world for her—one full of possibilities.

## Loneliness and Questioning

Because Wilma was sick so much, she was often home alone. Whenever her sisters and brothers went out, she was left behind. Feeling alone and rejected, Wilma cried a lot and drifted off into her own world. If it had not been for the kindness of a local black doctor, Wilma might never have had the courage to overcome her disability. With his encouragement, she learned to fight her illness. The doctor often told her: "Wilma, everything is gonna turn out all right. You just fight this thing, you understand?"

At first, Wilma questioned why she was so sick and why other children made fun of her. Then she began to think about how she could get kids to like her and play with her. "I think I started acquiring a competitive spirit right then and there," she said, "a spirit that would make me successful in sports later on. I was mad, and I was going to beat these illnesses no matter what. No more taking what came."

In remembering this time of her life, Wilma said: "All I really wanted back then was acceptance, to be accepted by the other kids as one of them. I couldn't get that, but in a way it was good for me. It made me determined to go beyond them, to do something someday that none of them would ever do, so then they'd have to accept me. But before I did anything else, I had to get myself healthy and into the neighborhood school."

Because of her illnesses, Wilma missed kindergarten and first grade. When she was seven years old, her parents enrolled her in the all-black elementary school in Clarksville. The school building was old, and the books and courses were not as good as those in the white school in town. But that didn't matter to Wilma. At last she was going to school and would be spending time with children her own age.

Wilma's teachers had a great influence upon her. Her first-grade teacher, Mrs. Allison, encouraged her to join a Brownie troop where girls took part in town activities and local parades. Wilma got a lot of attention from Mrs. Allison, who often asked her to help decorate the bulletin boards and make things for parties.

## A Teacher Makes a Difference

In fourth grade, Wilma learned fairness and responsibility from her teacher, Mrs. Hoskins—the hard way. It was the first spanking she ever got in her life. It was for not doing her homework. In Wilma's autobiography, she recalled these school memories. "The couple [of] swats didn't hurt; what hurt was inside, the feeling of knowing I had done something wrong and that it was important enough to be punished for."

Mrs. Hoskins also punished Wilma for daydreaming and for not paying attention. She would tell her: "Do it, Wilma. Don't daydream about it!" Eventually, Mrs. Hoskins' words made sense to Wilma. She went from daydreaming about the future to doing things to make the dreams come true. The hardest battle she would have to fight was the battle with herself. First she would have to get rid of the brace on her leg and get healthy.

## Walking without a Brace

Throughout the long ordeal of healing, Wilma watched her leg very carefully for the slightest improvement. She had a way of actually forcing the healing process along by secretly working on areas that seemed to be improving. Wilma even learned how to fake a no-limp walk so that her family and friends would think her leg was getting better. That way, she thought, people would think her leg was improving and be more willing to remove her brace when she asked them to. But in the end, she never asked her family to remove her brace. She just took it off herself.

One Sunday, when Wilma was nine and a half years old, she walked into church without her brace. What a surprise it was for her family and friends! From then on, she wore the brace only when her leg hurt or felt uncomfortable. Finally, when Wilma was twelve years old, she and her mother returned the brace to the hospital that had fitted her for it. That day was a turning point in Wilma's life. Without the brace, she felt free. And with her new sense of freedom, Wilma began to set goals for the future she had always dreamed about.

*Once Wilma could walk without her leg brace, she knew there was nothing she couldn't do.*

# NO GOAL TOO HIGH

**A**S A CHILD, Wilma knew very little about sports. She never played any kind of sport until high school. Wilma attended Burt High School in Clarksville, which included grades seven through twelve. The school had a girls' basketball team. Wilma's older sister Yvonne was on the team, so Wilma tried out for it too. Wilma was accepted on the team, but the coach didn't let her play for the first three seasons. However, Wilma made the most of the time she sat on the bench. She studied how the players rebounded and drew fouls.

She watched how referees enforced the rules. She even daydreamed about becoming a star on the team. Then, after each basketball season ended, Wilma went out for track, just for something to do.

In the ninth grade, Wilma took part in meets with other schools. She ran in the 50-, 75-, 100-, and 200-meter races, and on the relay team. She was a girl that was born to run, and she won every race that season on natural ability alone. But she still considered basketball her favorite sport.

Wilma was exceptionally tall for her age. At the end of the ninth grade, she was close to 6 feet (183 centimeters) tall and weighed only about 100 pounds (45 kg). She thought this was the perfect height and weight for the center or forward of a basketball team. Wilma practiced hard in her sophomore year in high school and finally won a starting position on the team as a guard. Later she also played forward.

Once during that season, she played a perfect game. With the whole school watching, she scored thirty-two points, making every one of the shots she tried. After that game, Wilma was quite a hero in the school. Getting recognition from her peers was important to her. All her life she had struggled to be accepted by others. Now she was not only accepted but also admired as a talented player. Wilma said, "I was somebody in school after that, for the first time."

## Coach Clinton Gray

But not everybody thought Wilma was a hero. Coach Clinton Gray expected Wilma to do her best. When she fell short of his expectations, he yelled at her in public. "Do it right and I won't have to yell," he would say. Wilma did not like being yelled at and quit the team several times because of it. When practice time came, however, she would show up and play harder than anybody else. Coach Gray was tough. He had high goals for the girls. He was dedicated to the game and wanted everyone who played for him to be dedicated too. The girls had to keep a "B" average in school, or they couldn't play on his team. Even when the girls practiced every day after school, Coach Gray asked 100 percent from them. He would let nothing interfere with basketball during the season!

The first season that Wilma played basketball, her team won eleven of their fifteen games. They won the Middle East Tennessee Conference title and qualified for a spot in the state tournament in

Nashville. The team clinched the first game of the tournament, with Wilma scoring 26 points. But they went into the second game a bit too cocky. After allowing several costly turnovers, the team lost. That loss ended the season for them. For Wilma, however, great things were just beginning. She would prove that there was no goal too high for her to reach once she set her mind to it.

During the state tournament, Wilma caught the attention of Edward S. Temple, a basketball referee and track coach at Tennessee State University in Nashville. Temple was impressed with Wilma's raw, natural ability. He saw potential in her and thought she might have a future in his sports program at Tennessee State. Temple talked with Coach Gray about setting up a program of jumping exercises for Wilma to strengthen her legs and extend her arm reach. Gray agreed with Temple's assessment and began working with Wilma. The exercises produced good results. Before long, Wilma was jumping higher and breaking her own records. The program also taught Wilma how to set goals for herself—and achieve them. She learned a valuable lesson in the process: practice makes perfect, and she would never excel without it.

## A Focus on Sports

Wilma's sophomore year was filled with typical teenage activities. She spent time with classmates at favorite neighborhood spots and went on dates with her boyfriend Robert Eldridge. Most of the time, however, she focused on sports. As soon as the basketball season ended, she turned her attention to track and field. Wilma enjoyed the sport, and she worked hard to excel in it. She believed that if she tried hard enough, she might even have a future in track.

Wilma ran every day. She was the first one out on the track in the morning and the last one to leave at night. Sometimes, Wilma even skipped classes to practice at the municipal stadium across the street. She liked to hang around the college teams and try to pick up valuable pointers. But after being called in to the principal's office and confronted with her misdeeds, Wilma stopped cutting classes.

The track program at Burt High School lacked funding. Coach Gray had only a small athletic budget to work with. The runners in his program did not have adequate equipment or a good track to practice on. Nevertheless, Wilma excelled in the sport. Even without formal training, she won every race she ran. Winning gave Wilma the confidence she needed to compete, but winning so often gave her a false sense of power. Wilma began to think no one could beat her. Unfortunately, she would find out how wrong she was. It was a hard lesson to learn—and one that she would never forget!

## A Disappointment

Even when the big meet of the year rolled around at the Tuskegee Institute in Alabama, and the best runners from the South were invited, Wilma thought she and her team would win easily. Coach Gray drove the team to Tuskegee. Before the race, Wilma was nervous, but confident. In fact, she was too confident. Wilma thought no one could possibly beat her. Unfortunately, she was no match for the well-trained, well-prepared athletes that ran against her. At the end of the day, Wilma had not won a single race or qualified for anything.

Shocked and ashamed, Wilma tried desperately to understand why she had lost. Later, reflecting on the race, she said: "After so many easy victories, using natural abilities alone, I got a false sense of being unbeatable." It was the shame of losing that ". . . brought me back down to earth and made me

*Tuskegee Institute in Alabama, where Rudolph competed in her first big meet*

realize that I couldn't do it on natural ability alone, that there was more to track than just running fast. I also realized it was going to test me as a person— could I come back and win again after being so totally crushed by a defeat?"

The next few months would test Wilma's resolve to win again. She was determined never to give up, no matter what happened. She knew that "nobody goes undefeated all the time. If you can pick up after a crushing defeat, and go on to win again, you are going to be a champion someday."

# WHAT MAKES A CHAMPION?

I N THE SPRING, Ed Temple drove down from Nashville to speak with Wilma's parents. He came to invite Wilma to spend the summer at Tennessee State University and train with other talented high-school track athletes. Wilma's parents thought carefully about Coach Temple's invitation. They considered the possibility that the coach's offer might turn into an an athletic scholarship that would enable their daughter to get a college education, which they could not afford. For the Rudolphs, this was a welcome opportunity. With this in mind, they graciously accepted the invitation and allowed their daughter to go to Nashville.

## A Summer Training Program

Saying good-bye to her family and her boyfriend, Robert, was not easy for Wilma. She would miss the comfort and security they provided. But the prospect of learning how to be a great runner overcame her fears. She actually felt excited about what the summer might hold.

Not long after settling into the dorm at Tennessee State University, Wilma began an intense routine of exercise and running 20 miles (32 km) a day, five days a week. The first two weeks of the program built up her endurance. The next part of the program taught her running techniques, such as how to breathe properly, how to keep her body relaxed, how to get off to a fast start, and how to plan a good strategy.

Competition among the girls was intense. They trained in teams. Coach Temple held a meet that summer so that the girls would get race experience. He kept scores and recorded the results. Wilma trained well but couldn't shake the problem she had with her starts. Her reflexes were slow, and her long legs made her starts awkward. She always lost speed coming out of the starting block. As a result, it took her longer to get going. Her first five or six strides were always off.

Improving her speed coming out of the starting block became one of Wilma's greatest challenges. Throughout her career, she had difficulty with this. However, she learned to compensate for a poor start by increasing her speed during the race and making up for the lost seconds.

## Training with Others

Training with other runners gave Wilma an important insight. She learned that each runner was unique and had her own particular problems to work out. For example, what was a problem for Wilma—the starting blocks—was not a problem for someone else. Learning about other runners' strengths and weaknesses helped Wilma to recognize her own strengths. It also helped her learn how to use the information to win a race. This knowledge was especially important to members of a relay team.

Coach Temple had set up a junior relay team that included Wilma. They spent the summer preparing to run in the National Amateur Athletic Union

*Coach Temple recognized Wilma's talent and pushed her to train hard and improve.*

(AAU) meet in Philadelphia, Pennsylvania, at the end of the summer. One of the ways they prepared was to get to know one another well. They learned how each member of the relay team moved, how they thought, and how they reacted. They watched one another run time and time again until they knew who was slow at the handoff and who could pick up speed to make up for lost seconds. They practiced the relay routine over and over again until it became automatic, until everything was precise.

At the end of the summer, Coach Temple and the relay team traveled north to Philadelphia to compete in the National AAU meet. It was Wilma's first visit to a big city. She was overwhelmed by its size. Wilma was entered in three events: the 75-yard dash, the 100-yard dash, and the 440-yard relay.

The first day, Wilma ran in nine races. She won both qualifying heats in the 75- and 100-yard dashes and went on to win the finals. She helped the relay team win both of its qualifying heats and then ace the final. The girls of Tennessee State swept the entire junior division of the National AAU meet and won the junior title! The victories boosted Wilma's

*Jackie Robinson was a great inspiration to Rudolph. He told her, "Don't let anything, or anybody, keep you from running."*

morale. She regained the confidence she had lost during her embarrassing loss at the Tuskegee Institute meet several months earlier.

## Meeting Jackie Robinson

An unexpected visit with Jackie Robinson, one of America's greatest baseball players, also helped Wilma get back on track. Robinson was the first African-American baseball player to play in the major leagues. In 1947, he signed on with the Brooklyn Dodgers. Until Robinson joined the Brooklyn Dodgers, African-American players were segregated to all-black teams in an all-black league. They received less pay and recognition in their careers than white players did.

During Robinson's visit with Wilma, they had a picture taken together. He complimented Wilma on her athletic abilities and told her: "Don't let anything, or anybody, keep you from running." These words inspired Wilma. Often they kept her from giving up when obstacles stood in her way. Robinson became Wilma's hero. She respected and admired him for his athletic abilities and for his courage in overcoming racial prejudice.

Shortly after the National AAU meet in Philadelphia, Coach Temple convinced Wilma to attend tryouts for the 1956 Olympic team in Seattle, Washington. Wilma knew little about the Olympic Games at the time. Nonetheless, she joined Coach Temple's group of college students at the tryouts. The girls nicknamed Wilma "Skeeter," because her long legs and arms made her look like a mosquito. At the time, Wilma was 6 feet (183 cm) tall and weighed only 89 pounds (40 kg). She was only sixteen years old and a junior in high school. Many of the other runners on Coach Temple's team were much more experienced than Wilma. The differences in age and experience often intimidated Wilma. Sometimes, during practice, she would hold back on her speed because she didn't want her teammates to be jealous of her ability.

## An Influential Teammate

One of her teammates was Mae Faggs, a champion runner. She had already won medals in the Olympics and held a variety of U.S. records in women's track. Mae took a special interest in Wilma and showed her how to build on her strengths as a runner. She helped her to stop doing things to get people to like her and to stop worrying about fitting in with everybody. With Mae's encouragement, Wilma made a decision that would affect her future success as a runner. She would no longer let what

*Coach Ed Temple (center) with the 1956 U.S. Olympic track and field team. Rudolph is at the far left.*

others thought of her determine how she would run. From then on, she would run for herself.

When the team arrived in Seattle, it was very cold. Because the girls were used to running in very hot weather, it took them several days to get adjusted. When Wilma saw the size of the stadium and the number of girls participating in the trials, she got sick to her stomach. Mae helped Wilma relax by getting her mind off her fears. She forced her to forget about the other runners in the race and focus her attention on herself and Mae. It worked. During the qualifying meet, Wilma raced as if only she and Mae were competing. After the race, Mae and Wilma learned they had come in first and second and qualified for the U.S. Olympic team!

Mae congratulated Wilma on her victory. She knew Wilma could have beaten her if she had wanted to. She told Wilma, "I think you've made it. You're ready to replace me right now. You really beat me in that race. What took you so long to get there? We've all known you had it in you, but we all wondered when it would come out. Today it did."

Qualifying for the Olympic team gave Wilma the confidence she needed to finally race for herself. Later in life she looked back at this event and said: "From that moment on, it seemed as if I wasn't afraid to challenge anybody anywhere. Whatever fears I had, fears of offending somebody by beating them, fears of being rejected by my teammates if I did too well, all of those fears vanished. My confidence as a runner had reached an all-time high, and my confidence as a person was improving too."

## "Olympic Mania"

Back home in Clarksville, people were caught up in "Olympic Mania." They were thrilled that Wilma would be competing in the Summer Olympics in Melbourne, Australia. A group of store owners gave her new luggage and clothes for the trip. Townspeople had a ceremony for her at the airport the day she left to begin the two-week Olympic training in Los Angeles. It was the first time Wilma had ever flown in an airplane.

In Los Angeles, the girls trained with Nel Jackson, the first female African-American coach of a U.S. Olympic team. They were pleased to be coached by an African-American woman and proud to represent the United States at the Olympics. For the first time, Wilma learned about the importance

*Nel Jackson helped Rudolph and the other team members train. She was the first female African-American coach of a U.S. Olympic team.*

of the Olympics and the meaning behind the five Olympic rings. The rings symbolize "the five continents linked together in friendly competition"— Africa, Asia, Australia, Europe, and the Americas. Those who had previously been in the Olympics told Wilma how much they had learned from traveling and meeting people of other cultures. They agreed that they valued the friendships they had made at the Olympic Village more than winning and getting medals.

At the conclusion of the two-week training camp, Wilma was running well. She was confident and ready as she boarded the plane for the two-day trip to Australia. The plane was packed with Olympic athletes. They stopped overnight in Hawaii and headed for the second stop of the flight—the Fiji Islands. What Wilma experienced on the trip was different from anything she had known in Tennessee. It was like a dream to a girl who had grown up in the segregated part of a small southern town in the United States and known no other way of life. Only a few years earlier, Wilma needed a brace to walk. Now, at age sixteen, she was flying to Australia to race in the Olympics with the best runners in the world.

# VICTORY BOUND

**O**CTOBER 1956, the first time she raced as an Olympian, was a month Wilma would never forget. Shortly after arriving in Melbourne, Wilma checked into the Olympic Village with her teammates. Immediately afterward, they began a weeklong preparation for the coming races. Between the long practices, the young athletes signed autographs and made friends from all over the world. It was a special and exciting time for all of them, but Wilma and her teammates missed Coach Temple. Their concentration was less than perfect without the security of his presence and the strength of his advice.

Wilma ran her first race three days into the games. She finished third in the 200-meter dash, qualifying her to run in the semifinals. In the semifinals she came in third once again. However, only

*Practicing for the relay in Melbourne. This event would make the U.S. women famous.*

the top two could compete in the finals, so Wilma was eliminated from the 200-meter event. Wilma had expected to do better and was devastated when she lost the opportunity to compete in the final 200. Feeling that she had let down everybody in the United States, Wilma couldn't eat or sleep for several days.

However, she overcame her disappointment and returned to the Olympic stadium a few days later to watch the 100- and 200-meter finals. Betty Cuthbert, an eighteen-year-old Australian runner, won gold medals in the 100-and 200-meter dashes for three gold medals. Wilma would later say of Betty Cuthbert's victory, "Watching her win those gold medals motivated me into making a commitment to do the very same thing someday. I was determined that four years from then, no matter where the Olympics were held, I was going to be there and I was going to win a gold medal or two for the United States."

Betty Cuthbert's win snapped Wilma out of her bad mood. When it came time for her to run in the women's 400-meter relay, Wilma's competitive spirit emerged. She ran with a renewed commitment to bring home a medal for the United States. In the 400-meter relay, Wilma and her three teammates

*Australian runner Betty Cuthbert. Her success at the 1956 Olympic Games ignited Wilma's competitive spirit.*

each ran 100 meters, and then handed a 12-inch (30-cm) baton to the next teammate. Mae Faggs, the strongest starter, ran first. Wilma ran third. The team ran a nice clean race and finished in third place. The American team was not expected to win, but they proved the experts wrong. They captured the bronze medal!

Wilma left the Olympic Games proud that she had accomplished at least part of what she had set out to do. Although Wilma had not qualified for the 100- and 200-meter finals, she had gained valuable Olympic experience. And her team was taking home bronze medals for a third-place finish in the 400-meter relay. Before leaving the Olympic Village, Wilma set a new goal—to return in four years and win gold!

## Back in Clarksville

When Wilma arrived home in Clarksville in November, Coach Temple was waiting to congratulate her. Burt High School hosted a special assembly to honor her. Following the assembly, Wilma played on the girls' basketball team in its first game of the season. After that night, Wilma continued to help her team to victory. At the end of the season, the team looked

*Showing off their bronze medals. The 1956 team placed third in the 400-meter relay event.*

back with pride. They had won every game and won the state tournament for the second year in a row. It was the first girls' team in Tennessee to score more than 100 points a game. But Wilma did not feel very successful. Ever since returning from the Olympics, she felt as if people were treating her differently.

Even though Wilma averaged 35 points a game, people didn't seem to be satisfied with her accomplishments. Wilma felt that no matter what she did, it was not enough. More was always expected of her. Adjusting to the way the coaches and teammates related to her also posed a problem for Wilma. Because of her Olympic status, players now seemed to be intimidated by her. They were not themselves when they were around her. Wilma felt as though the coach was harder on her than on the others and pointed out her mistakes more often.

As these pressures mounted, Wilma turned to her closest friends for comfort. She began to spend more time with her boyfriend, Robert Eldridge, whom she had known ever since first grade. Wilma and Robert had a lot in common. Robert excelled in sports. He was a star athlete in basketball and football. He and Wilma were a popular couple in high school. Unfortunately, their intimacy brought responsibilities that neither one of them was ready to accept.

## An Unexpected Complication

At the beginning of her senior year, Wilma went to see the doctor for her annual preseason physical exam. She found out that she was going to have a baby and that Robert was the father. Wilma was afraid of what her parents would say and how her pregnancy would affect her future in sports. Fortunately, Wilma's parents were very understanding and supported her decision to have the baby. Robert asked Wilma to marry him but Wilma's father forbade her to see Robert again. So marriage was out of the question.

Wilma's parents thought Wilma and Robert were too young to get married and that Wilma was not ready to be a mother. After serious discussions about the problem, they came up with a solution they hoped would be the best for everyone. Wilma's sister Yvonne agreed to care for the baby until Wilma could be a full-time mother. Yvonne was married and living in St. Louis, Missouri, with her husband and five-year-old son at the time. While her son was in school, Yvonne would have time to care for the newborn. Wilma and her parents know that the baby would be in good hands

## Off to College

In June 1958, Wilma graduated from high school. In July, she gave birth to a baby girl—Yolanda. Shortly after Yolanda's birth, Yvonne took the baby to St. Louis. Wilma returned to school and resumed training with Coach Temple.

Although Coach Temple had a rule barring mothers from his program at Tennessee State, he made an exception for Wilma. He said that as long as Wilma's family cared for the baby, Wilma could participate. So in the fall, Wilma began college at Tennessee State on a full athletic scholarship. Her major was elementary education and her minor was psychology.

Coach Temple set high standards in his program. All the participants had to maintain a B-average in their courses. Wilma found the course work and training requirements very heavy. She had a difficult time adjusting to studying such long hours. And after studying and training, she had little time or energy for other activities. Yet Wilma managed to meet all the requirements of Coach Temple's program. One thing about college she did not count on, however, was how much she would miss her baby Yolanda.

During Wilma's first Christmas break, she returned to Clarksville, where she secretly met Robert. They drove to St. Louis to bring Yolanda back to Clarksville. With the baby living in Clarksville, Wilma counted on having more time to spend with her. The new arrangement was good for Wilma. That year, she learned how to juggle her responsibilities as a student, a member of the track team, and a mother. After much hard work, she made the track team her freshman year. She was a Tigerbelle at last!

## Training for Another Olympics

Early in 1960, Wilma began training seriously for the Olympics, which were to be held in Rome, Italy, in September of that year. First, she participated in a preliminary race—the National AAU meet in Corpus Christi, Texas. That race decided who would be invited to the Olympic trials at Texas Christian University a few weeks later. Wilma ran well in the Nationals. She ran a 22.9 in the 200 meters—the fastest 200 meters ever run by a woman. Having set

*When Rudolph qualified for the 1960 Olympic team, she knew she was ready for the competition.*

*Stretching at the 1960 Olympic Games. Rudolph had to prepare both mentally and physically before each race.*

a new world record, Wilma knew she was ready for the Olympic trials.

In August, Wilma won both the 100- and 200-meter dashes at the U.S. Olympic trials and qualified for the Olympic team. She was delighted when Ed Temple was selected as the coach of the U.S. women's track team.

For three weeks, Coach Temple worked the team hard at Kansas State University in Emporia. Then the team spent a week in New York City getting measured and fitted for Olympic uniforms and equipment. The team arrived in Rome two weeks before the start of the games, which gave them sufficient time to practice.

In Rome, the temperature was a scorching 100°F (38°Celsius). Many of the athletes found the heat unbearable, but Wilma was used to Tennessee summers and had little problem with the humidity. The weather presented no obstacle for her, but an unsuspected hole in the ground threatened to destroy her opportunity to race. The day before Wilma was scheduled to run her first race, she went jogging. While crossing a field, she stepped into a small hole and twisted her ankle. Rumors spread wildly throughout the Olympic village that she had broken her ankle and would not be able to run. Fortunately, the ankle was only sprained. After having her ankle taped tightly and packed in ice, Wilma went to bed. The following morning, she was ready to run.

Wilma ran the 100- and 200-meter dashes without a problem and qualified for the finals. During the 100-meter qualifying race, she tied the world record: 11.3 seconds. In the finals, she beat her world record time by three-tenths of a second, winning by an astonishing 11 seconds flat.

Wilma's run would have set a new world record, if it had not been for the speed of the wind that day. Authorities said that because of the wind speed, and the fact that Wilma was racing with the wind at her back, she had a slight advantage over previous runners. (The official limit was 2.0 meters per second. On the day Wilma ran, the wind was measured at 2.752 meters.) As a result, Olympic authorities would not compare Wilma's final time with previous records set on a less windy day.

Wilma was disappointed with the ruling but thrilled with the results of her races. She had little

*Receiving the gold medal for the 100-meter dash. Rudolph would win two other gold medals as well.*

*Getting off to a good start. Rudolph tied a world record in a qualifying heat for the 100-meter sprint.*

time to enjoy the sweet taste of victory, however. She was too busy focusing on the challenge of her next race, the 200-meter sprint. Expectations ran high as Wilma left the starting block in a mist of light rain. Although the rain slowed Wilma down, she did not disappoint the crowd, who had been anticipating another record win. In the qualifying round, Wilma crossed the finish line with a time of 23.2 seconds. In the final round, she passed all her competitors, winning with a time of 24.0 seconds. Wilma was pleased with her win but disappointed with her time. During practice, she had been finishing at a consistent 22.9 seconds.

Wilma's final race, the 400-meter relay, took place on the last day of the Olympics. It was an exceptionally hot day. All eyes were on Wilma, who by this time had become a crowd favorite. The fans chanted her name and shouted their support. Wilma's ankle was bothering her, but she would not let it affect her concentration. She knew that she had a key position in the race. As the anchor, or final runner, her run would decide the race.

Great Britain, the former Soviet Union, and West Germany were favored to win the relay. For the U.S. team to steal the win, it would have to get off to a fast start and run without mistakes. That's just what the U.S. team planned to do. During the first two legs of the race, the U.S. women followed the plan well. As the third runner completed the course, however, and handed Wilma the baton, Wilma fumbled it. She regained a firm grip of the baton without

*Rudolph (center) with the second- and third-place finishers in the 200-meter race*

dropping it, but lost precious seconds in the process. Two runners on the opposing teams passed her.

Determined to make up the time she had lost, Wilma increased her speed. In the final stretch, she still lagged 2 meters (6.5 feet) behind the Russian

*Crossing the finish line. Rudolph ran the last leg of the 400-meter relay at the 1960 Olympic Games.*

sprinter. Using every ounce of strength she had, Wilma lunged forward at the finish line and then fell to the ground, exhausted. The race was a photo finish. Olympic officials had to examine the photographs taken at the finish line to determine who had won.

When the announcement came that the U.S. team had won the gold by three-tenths of a second, the crowd went wild. The Americans had set a new record time of 44.5 seconds, and Wilma had become the first American woman to win three gold medals at a Summer Olympics.

## "The Tennessee Tornado"

Wilma and her teammates remained in Europe for several weeks, racing in several cities. At the British Empire Games in London, England, Wilma won two events: the 100 meters and the relay. Fans and reporters mobbed Wilma wherever she went. Reporters called her "the Tennessee Tornado." Everyone wanted to take her picture and interview her. Some countries had their own favorite name for Wilma. In Italy, they called her *La Gazella Nera* (the Black Gazelle). In France they called her *La Perle Noire* (the Black Pearl).

All the special attention Wilma was receiving began to take its toll on the team. A few of her teammates felt ignored by the press and began taking it out on Wilma. Their poor sportsmanship even affected their ability to run well as a team. During a 440-yard relay race, the team ran poorly. When it came time for Wilma to begin the final 100 meters of the race, her team was already 40 yards (37 m) behind the other runners. Refusing to give up, Wilma ran the fastest anchor leg of her life to close the gap and win the race. The crowd gave her a standing ovation.

After the close of the Olympics, the U.S. team traveled to Stuttgart, Germany, to participate in an invitational meet featuring Olympic winners. Wilma ran well in Europe. She won the 100 meters in Germany, as well as the 100 meters in the Netherlands a few weeks later. Publicly, Wilma was a star, but privately, jealous teammates were ignoring her and refusing to even talk to her. Hurt by their behavior, homesick, and tired, Wilma was anxious to go home.

## Back in Nashville

Wilma breathed a sigh of relief as she stepped off the plane in Nashville, Tennessee, to cheering crowds. Even the governor and mayor were there to greet

*Happy to be home. Rudolph is greeted by her mom (left), dad, and sister Charlene (right) after returning from the 1960 Olympics.*

her. The band played while reporters impatiently waited to interview her. The Clarksville parade started 2 miles (3.2 km) outside the town. Wilma rode into Clarksville in a police motorcade. The streets were lined with thousands of cheering peo-

*The people of Clarksville had a parade to celebrate Rudolph's success at the Olympic Games.*

ple. For the first time in Clarksville history, both white and black citizens had turned out to honor one of their own. They congratulated Wilma and showed her how proud they were of their hometown girl. The parade and the banquet that followed were the first racially integrated events ever held in Clarksville.

Wilma never forgot what her accomplishments meant to the townspeople, or how her life began to change because of them. One memorable speech, given by an elderly white judge at Wilma's banquet, had a great impact on the audience. "Ladies and gentlemen," he said, "you play a piano. You can play very nice music on a piano by playing only the black keys on it, and you can play very nice music on the same piano by playing only the white keys on it. But ladies and gentlemen, the absolute best music comes out of that piano when you play both the black keys and the white keys together."

## Touring the United States

News of Wilma's Olympic fame spread across the country. For weeks she toured cities, giving speeches. In Chicago, Mayor Richard J. Daley gave her the keys to the city. In Washington, D.C., she visited President John F. Kennedy in the White

*During her post-Olympics tour of the country, Rudolph met many important people including President John F. Kennedy.*

*Receiving the James E. Sullivan Award. Presenting the honor to Rudolph is Louis J. Fisher of the Amateur Athletic Union.*

House. Wilma was the first woman to be invited to run in meets previously open only to men—the New York Athletic Club meet, the Millrose Games, the Los Angeles Times Games, the Penn Relays, and the Drake Relays. Ever since then, the doors have been open to women.

In 1961, Wilma received the James E. Sullivan Award for the amateur athlete who does the most "to advance good sportsmanship throughout the year." She was named Woman Athlete of the Year by the Associated Press for 1960 and 1961 and "Sportsman of the Year" by the European Sportswriters Organization. This was the first time the "Sportsman of the Year" award had been given to a woman. In 1960, Wilma also became the first American to receive the Christopher Columbus Award from Italy for being the Most Outstanding International Sports Personality.

Wherever Wilma toured, her expenses were paid for and all her decisions were made for her. Life seemed wonderful. As Wilma later said, "Everybody was making decisions for me; I never had to think about anything else but looking pretty and smiling a lot."

At the time, Wilma didn't realize that all the attention and pampering she was getting was only temporary. It wouldn't lead to a profitable future. The people who sponsored Wilma's trips were making money from her appearances, but Wilma wasn't making a cent. In those days, black amateur athletes had no managers to protect their rights and help them make an income from their career. So, after all the tours were over, Wilma found herself on her own, without an income or the security of a stable career outside of sports.

# A TEACHER
# AT HEART

**A**FTER RETURNING TO Clarksville, Wilma went back to college to finish her degree in elementary education. As an amateur athlete, Wilma couldn't accept money for racing so she took a part-time job at the university post office. Now and then she appeared in public and accepted invitations to race. In February 1961, she tied her own world record for the 60-yard dash in New York City at the Millrose Games, which were previously open only to men.

Track and field had always been considered a "man's sport" and was limited to males. But Wilma's dominance in the sport helped to change all that. She paved the way for other women runners. In the sport of women's track and field, she became a hero.

For the next two years, Wilma took every opportunity to travel and race. To everyone's surprise, she didn't win every race she ran. She lost from time to time. People's expectations of her were often unreasonable. They expected her to be superhuman, and when she lost, sometimes their comments were cruel.

## A Final Race

In 1962, Wilma accepted an invitation from Stanford University in Los Angeles, California, to run in a meet with athletes from the former Soviet Union. While Wilma trained for the race, she thought seriously about making it her last race. Realizing that she could not run forever, Wilma thought it would be best to retire when she was running well. More important, she wanted to marry Robert and create the family that her daughter needed. But deciding to concentrate on a family meant that she would have to retire.

At Stanford, Wilma won the 100-meter dash and

*Rudolph lost a close race in 1962 to fellow Olympic teammate Jean Holmes.*

then anchored the 400-meter relay team. She came from behind to pass the lead runner and win. Later, Wilma said she remembered thinking, "That was it. I knew it. The crowd in the stadium was on its feet, giving me a standing ovation, and I knew what time it was. Time to retire, with a sweet taste." For Wilma, leaving her sport as a winner was a great way to finish her career. She said, ". . . I wanted to go out on top, even if it meant going out a little earlier than I should have. Better go out early and on top, I figured, than too late and beaten."

After Wilma's final race, a little boy approached her and asked her for her autograph. Wilma's response became part of a legend about her. She answered, "Son . . . I'll do one better than that." Then, she untied her shoes, autographed them, and gave them to the little boy. According to legend, that's how her track career officially ended.

## Awards, Honors, and Family

Shortly after Wilma retired in 1962, she received the Babe Zaharias Award for being the world's most outstanding female athlete. In May 1963, she served as a U.S. representative at the Games of Friendship in

*Receiving the Babe Zaharias Award in 1962. Presenting it to her is George Zaharias, Babe's husand.*

Dakar, Senegal, the largest track-and-field event ever held in Africa. She also went to Japan with evangelist Billy Graham as a member of the Baptist Christian Athletes.

A few months later, Wilma received her degree in elementary education, and she and Robert were married. They had an outdoor wedding in an open field, near the projects, or public housing development, where Wilma's mother grew up. Wilma and Robert couldn't afford a honeymoon. Instead, they went to Robert's family reunion, where Wilma met all his relatives.

Shortly after the wedding, life returned to normal for Wilma. She and Robert finally began the family life they had always talked about. In the fall, Robert enrolled in Tennessee State University to get his degree. Wilma began teaching second grade at the school in Clarksville that she had attended when she was a child. She also became coach of the track-and-field team at Burt High School, replacing Coach Gray who had been killed in an automobile accident earlier that year.

Financially, Wilma and Robert were on shaky ground. They were relying on Wilma's income as a teacher to provide for their family. At the time, they could not count on receiving any money for her appearances as a famous athlete.

In today's world, she would have earned a great deal of money making commercials and endorsing products. But a black woman athlete in the early 1960s had little opportunity for profit from her sport. Once Wilma said: "I knew that, since 1960, I had been a good wife and mother, but I was besieged with money problems; people were always expecting me to be a star, but I wasn't making the money to live like one. I felt exploited both as a woman and as a black person, and this bothered me very much."

## Beginning a New Career

Wilma began her career eager to put into practice the exciting teaching ideas she had learned in college. The new methods, however, met with disinterest and even resistance. After a brief attempt to establish herself as a teacher, Wilma quit her job. During her career as a teacher, Wilma gave birth to her second daughter, Djuanna. In 1965, her first son, Robert, was born. After Wilma left teaching, she moved from job to job, trying to find a position that would provide a good income for her family and

*Wilma Rudolph graduated from college in 1963 with a degree in elementary education.*

measure up to the image and prestige she was used to as an athlete.

First the family moved to Evansville, Indiana, where Wilma became director of a community center. After only a year, they moved again to Poland Springs, Maine, where Wilma took charge of girls' physical education for a government-sponsored program.

In 1967, Vice President Hubert Humphrey asked her to participate in "Operation Champ"—a government-sponsored program that trained young inner-city athletes. Thinking that at last she could help others make their dreams come true, Wilma eagerly gave of her time and talent. She joined other athletes and traveled to various cities to train children.

Wilma hoped that helping inner-city children to gain self-confidence and find success in sports would help eliminate poverty and racial prejudice. But change comes slowly, and Wilma saw little results from her work. She was appalled by the oppression of inner-city life. She knew firsthand what poverty was like because she had grown up in it but her experience was nothing like the poverty of the ghettos. Looking back on this period of her life, Wilma wrote: "I grew up in a small, segregated

*Rudolph talking to reporters in 1969 during a trip to Rome. Years after her Olympic fame, she still had many things she wished to accomplish.*

southern town, but the oppression there was nothing compared to the oppression I saw in the big-city black ghettos."

Shortly after the assignment with Operation Champ ended, Wilma was transferred to the Job Corps center in St. Louis. Wilma then took a teaching job at a junior high school in Detroit for about a year and a half. Though Wilma was always a teacher at heart, she could not find real fulfillment in it.

She said: ". . . I felt I wanted more out of life for myself and my family. Eight years had gone by since I won the three gold medals in the Olympics, and I still hadn't found the fulfillment outside of track that I had found in it."

Depressed about her situation, Wilma accepted from the owner of an Italian newspaper an all-expenses-paid trip to tour Italy. She also served briefly as a commentator for West German television and radio. By returning to Europe, Wilma thought that she might recapture some of the past glory of her Olympic days. Instead of gaining peace of mind from her visit to Europe, however, Wilma was frustrated by Europeans taking advantage of her fame. They used her status for their own purposes.

Shortly after returning from Europe, Wilma took

a job at the University of California, Los Angeles as an administrator of the Afro-American Studies program. The job didn't last long, and she moved her family to Chicago. In Chicago, Wilma directed athletic programs for Mayor Daley's Youth Foundation. That job, too, soon came to an end.

## Wilma Unlimited

In 1971, Wilma gave birth to her second son, Xurry. In the late 1970s, she worked as a public-relations spokeswoman for a bank and did occasional fashion modeling. But always, Wilma believed that she was hired for what her name and celebrity status would bring to a project—never for her skills or abilities.

Finally, she realized that she had to take control of her own life. She couldn't rely on others to give her the perfect job or the perfect title. So, rather than feel exploited by her employers, Wilma started her own company. She called it "Wilma Unlimited." The company gave her opportunities to travel, lecture, and support special causes. No longer did she have to answer to the pressures and demands of others. One journalist called Wilma's company "a one-woman corporation."

*Rudolph with her daughter Yolanda. For a time, the young girl aspired to run in her mother's footsteps.*

*With her family. Rudolph (seated) was inducted into the National Track and Field Hall of Fame in 1974.*

## Influencing Others

Throughout her life, Wilma had many obstacles to overcome. But those struggles never made her bitter or selfish. Instead, she felt honored to be able to share her knowledge with others. She enjoyed giving of herself to other athletes and providing advice when she could.

Rudolph especially inspired young African-American female athletes. Once such athlete was Florence Griffith Joyner, the next woman to win three gold medals in one Olympics. That happened in 1988.

"It was a great thrill for me to see," Rudolph said. "I thought I'd never get to see that. Florence Griffith Joyner—every time she ran, I ran."

Jackie Joyner-Kersee, a winner of six Olympic medals, said, "She was always in my corner. If I had a problem, I could call her at home. It was like talking to someone you knew for a lifetime." Bob Kersee, husband and coach of Jackie Joyner-Kersee, said Rudolph was the greatest influence for African-American women athletes that he has ever known.

# PASSING THE BATON

I N 1977, WILMA wrote her autobiography—*Wilma*. The same year, a made-for-TV movie based on the book was produced. Wilma served as a consultant during the filming.

The movie was produced by NBC and starred Shirley Jo Finney as Wilma. Denzel Washington and Cicely Tyson were members of the cast as well. The book and movie provided inspiration to physically challenged people who may have felt trapped by their conditions. As a public speaker she was in great demand. In 1980, she was named to

*Wilma Rudolph took time to work with Shirley Jo Finney during the filming of* Wilma, *the 1977 television movie about her life.*

the Women's Sports Hall of Fame. Throughout the 1980s, Wilma toured extensively.

In 1981, Wilma started the Wilma Rudolph Foundation, dedicated to nurturing talented young athletes. In its prime, the foundation assisted more than 1,000 prospective athletes. They received help in preparing for amateur track meets, national sports festivals, and the Olympics. The foundation also followed every trainee's progress in school. The foundation promoted education as well as sports ability, preparing athletes for a career on and off the athletic field. Wilma spoke from experience when she said: "Many think that if they make it big as an athlete their worries are over. I'm here to tell you that they're just beginning."

Wilma was proud of her work with inner-city young people. "I tell them that the most important aspect is to be yourself and have confidence in yourself," she said. "I remind them the triumph can't be had without the struggle."

## More Awards and Recognition

In 1983, Wilma was awarded the Vitalis Cup for Sports Excellence. In 1984, the Women's Sports

*Race car driver Janet Guthrie (left) with Rudolph at the Women's Sports Hall of Fame*

Foundation named her one of America's five "Greatest Woman Athletes," along with runner Mary Decker and tennis stars Martina Navratilova, Chris Evert, and Billie Jean King.

Wilma did much to promote women's sports in America. She lobbied to pass Title IX, the law requiring equal treatment for women in college sports. She also helped establish the USA Track and Field Hall of Fame in Charleston, West Virginia. The hall is now located in Indianapolis.

## A Legacy

During her lifetime, Wilma paved the way for the talented black women athletes who came after her. Many of them were inspired by her example and took part in programs sponsored by her foundation. At the time Wilma excelled in track and field, black women athletes were on the bottom rung of the ladder in American sports. By the time Wilma established her foundation, however, black women athletes were beginning to move up.

When Wilma's daughter Yolanda became interested in running, Wilma told her how difficult it would be to run as Wilma Rudolph's daughter. Wilma was ready to "pass the baton" to her only if

*Holding a photograph of herself at the 1960 Olympic Games.
Rudolph's life was one of both struggles and good memories.*

Yolanda was ready to run on her own terms. Knowing how demanding the press would be, Wilma counseled Yolanda: "Don't try to live up to anything. Be yourself and you'll do fine." Yolanda, however, did not pursue the sport beyond her years at Tennessee State.

## Endings

In 1993, President Bill Clinton honored her with a National Sports Award. She was the only woman to receive the award. The other recipients were Arnold Palmer, Kareem Abdul-Jabbar, Muhammad Ali, and Ted Williams. The group was known as "the Great Ones" of sports.

Wilma was only fifty-four years old when she died of cancer on November 12, 1994. She had been in and out of hospitals for several months after brain cancer was diagnosed. She died in her home in Nashville, Tennessee.

Leroy Walker, president of the U.S. Olympic Committee, said, "All of us recognize that this is obviously a tremendous loss. Wilma was still very much involved with a number of Olympic programs. It's a tragic loss. She was struck with an illness that, unfortunately, we can't do very much about."

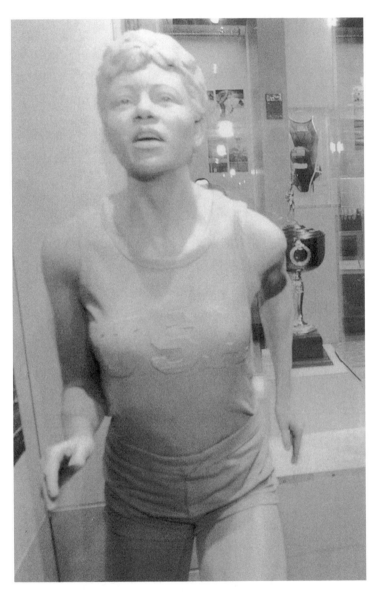

*A statue of Wilma Rudolph at the Tennessee Sports Hall of Fame*

Her death, like her birth, was premature. We will never know the extent to which her contributions as a public speaker, teacher, community and business leader, and role model for the disabled might have affected the lives of young athletes. However, we do know how her hard work, determination, and strength of character determined the outcome of her own life. We need only look at her accomplishments to judge their effect.

On August 11, 1995, the new Wilma G. Rudolph Residence Center at Tennessee State University was dedicated to its famous former student. It is a six-story residence center for women. At the dedication, Dr. James Hefner, president of Tennessee StateUniversity, said, "Wilma Rudolph was an example to us in not only winning in sports, but she also taught us the meaning of triumphing over the odds and winning at life. Because of the strength of character with which she faced life's challenges, we are indeed proud and honored to dedicate Tennessee State University's newest residence center in her name."

The legendary Edward Temple, Wilma's former coach, also spoke at the dedication. He said, "The center is certainly named after a classy young lady. It's a great tribute. Wilma would have been awfully happy that such a magnificent structure was named in her honor." Although Wilma did not live to see the center completed, she saw it under construction before she died. Wilma was proud of the building and commented on its beauty. It is a fitting tribute to Wilma Rudolph's life and to her remarkable legacy. What's even more remarkable is that the center will provide opportunities for thousands of women to carry on the Rudolph legacy in the future.

When asked how she would like to be remembered one day, Wilma Rudolph replied: "I would be disappointed if I was only remembered as a runner, because I feel my contribution to the youth of America has far exceeded the woman who was the Olympic champion."

# TIMELINE

| | |
|---|---|
| **1940** | Wilma Rudolph born on June 23 in Clarksville, Tennessee |
| **1945** | Is stricken with polio |
| **1946** | Begins going to a hospital in Nashville for regular treatments for her condition |
| **1947** | Finally starts elementary school |
| **1952** | Returns her leg brace to the hospital after learning to walk without them |
| **mid-50s** | Plays basketball and runs track in high school |
| **1956** | Trains with other high school track athletes at Tennessee State University; attends National AAU meet in Philadelphia; competes in the Olympic Games in Melbourne, Australia, and wins a bronze medal in the 400-meter relay |
| **1957** | Realizes that she is pregnant |
| **1958** | Graduates from high school in June; gives birth to a daughter, Yolanda, in July; enrolls at Tennessee State University in the fall |

| | |
|---|---|
| **1960** | Sets a new world record in the 200-meter race at National AAU meet in Corpus Cristi; competes in the Olympic Games in Rome, Italy, and wins three gold medals; is named Woman Athlete of the Year by the Associated Press; receives the Christopher Columbus Award from Italy |
| **1961** | Is named Woman Athlete of the Year for a second time; receives the James E. Sullivan Award |
| **1962** | Retires from racing; receives the Babe Zaharias Award |
| **1963** | Serves as a U.S. representative the Games of Friendship in Dakar, Senegal; graduates from college; marries longtime boyfriend, Robert Eldridge; begins teaching second grade |
| **1964** | Gives birth to another daughter, Djuanna |
| **1965** | Gives birth to a son, Robert |
| **late '60s** | Holds a series of jobs but is dissatisfied by them |
| **1971** | Gives birth to a second son, Xurry |
| **early '70s** | Creates her own company, "Wilma Unlimited" |
| **1977** | Publishes her autobiography, *Wilma* |
| **1980** | Is named to the Women's Sports Hall of Fame |
| **1981** | Begins the Wilma Rudolph Foundation |
| **1983** | Is awarded the Vitalis Cup for Sports Excellence |
| **1984** | Is named as one of America's five "Greatest Woman Athletes" |
| **1994** | Dies of cancer on November 12 |

# HOW TO BECOME AN ATHLETE

## The Job

Amateur athletes play or compete for titles or trophies, but not for money. Professional athletes in sports such as tennis, figure-skating, golf, running, or boxing, compete for money and prizes.

In tennis and boxing, an athlete may compete against one person. In some sports, such as figure skating, golf, and cycling, an athlete may compete against six to thirty people. In certain individual events, such as the New York Marathon, tens of thousands of runners may compete.

The winners of individual sports are evaluated differently. For example, the winner of a foot race is the one who crosses the finish line first. In tennis the winner is the player who wins the most games in a given number of sets. In boxing and figure skating, a panel of judges chooses the winners. Competitions are organized by groups who promote the sport. In a professional sport, different levels of competition are based on age, ability, and gender. There are often different designations and events within one sport. Tennis, for example, consists of doubles and singles, while track-and-field contains many different events.

Athletes train year-round. Some work on their own. Others work with a coach, friend, parent, or trainer. In addition to stretching and exercising specific muscles, athletes develop eating and sleeping habits that help them stay in top condition throughout the year. Most professional athletes train all year. They vary the type and duration of their workouts to develop strength, flexibility, and speed. They also work on technique and control. Often, an athlete's training focuses on specific details of the game or program. For example, figure skaters may concentrate on jumps, turns, and hand movements. Similarly, sprinters vary their workouts to include some distance work, some sprints, weight training, and maybe some mental exercises to build control and focus while in the starter's blocks. Tennis players spend hours practicing particular shots.

## Requirements

*High School*  A high-school diploma provides the basic skills needed to become a professional athlete. Business and mathematics classes teach you how to manage money wisely. Speech classes help you become a better communicator. Physical-education classes help build strength, agility, and competitive spirit. You should, of course, participate in every organized sport that interests you.

In some individual sports, such as tennis and gymnastics, some competitors are high-school students.

Teenagers in this situation often have private coaches. Many practice before and after school, while others are home-schooled as they travel to competitions.

*Postsecondary* There are no formal education requirements for sports, but certain opportunities are available only to students in four-year colleges and universities. Many athletes develop their skills in college-level competitions. Outstanding ability in athletics enables many students to obtain a college education. An education is always a wise investment.

*Other Requirements* So much competition exists among athletes in any given sport that talent alone is not the primary requirement. Perseverance, hard work, ambition, and courage are all essential qualities for the individual who dreams of becoming a professional athlete. "If you want to be a pro, there's no halfway. There's no three-quarters way," says Eric Roller, a former professional tennis player. Other requirements vary according to the sport. Jockeys, for example, are usually small-boned men and women.

## Exploring

If you are interested in pursuing a career in professional sports, you should start participating in that sport as much and as early as possible. An individual may be too old at fifteen to realistically begin pursuing a professional career in some sports. By playing the sport and by talking to coaches, trainers, and athletes in the field, you can learn whether you like the sport enough to make it a career and whether you have enough talent. You can also learn a lot about the sport. You can contact professional organizations and associations for information on how to best prepare for a career in a particular sport. Some specialized training programs are available. The best way to find out about them is to get in touch with the organizations that promote the sport.

## Employers

Professional athletes in individual sports do not work for employers. They choose the competitions or tournaments they wish to enter. For example, a professional runner may choose to run in the Boston Marathon and then travel to Atlanta for the Peachtree Road Race.

## Starting Out

Professional athletes must meet the requirements established by the groups that organize their sport. Sometimes this means meeting a physical standard, such as age, height, or weight; and sometimes it means participating in a certain number of competitions. Professional organizations usually arrange it so that athletes can build up their skills by taking part in lower-level competitions. College sports are an excellent way to improve one's skills while pursuing an education.

## Advancement

Professional athletes get ahead in their sport by working and practicing hard, and by winning. Professional athletes usually have agents who make deals for them, such as which team they will play for and how much they will be paid. These agents may also be involved with the athlete's commercial endorsements, taxes, and financial investments.

A college education can prepare all athletes for the

day when their bodies can no longer compete at the top level. Every athlete should be prepared to move into another career.

## Earnings

Salaries, cash prizes, and commercial endorsements vary from sport to sport. A lot depends on the popularity of the sport and its ability to attract fans. Still other sports, like boxing, depend on the skill of the fight's promoters to create interest in the fight. An elite professional tennis player who wins Wimbledon, for example, usually earns more than half a million dollars in a matter of two weeks. Add to that the incredible sums a Wimbledon-champion can make in endorsements and the tennis star is earning over one million dollars a year. This scenario is misleading, however; to begin with, top athletes usually cannot perform at such a level for very long, which is why a good accountant and investment counselor comes in handy. Second, for every top athlete who earns millions of dollars in a year, there are hundreds of professional athletes who earn less than $40,000. The stakes are incredibly high, the competition fierce.

The financial success of an athlete may depend greatly on the individual's character or personality. An athlete who has a nasty temper or is known to behave badly may be able to win games but may not be able to cash in on the commercial endorsements. Advertisers are careful whom they choose to endorse products. Some athletes have lost million-dollar accounts because of bad behavior on or off the field.

Many athletes go into some area of coaching, sports administration, management, or broadcasting. The professional athlete's insight can be a great asset in these careers. Some athletes simultaneously pursue interests completely unrelated to their sport, such as education, business, social welfare, or the arts. Many enjoy coaching young people or volunteering with local school teams.

## Work Environment

Athletes compete in many kinds of conditions. Track-and-field athletes often compete in hot or rainy conditions but officials can call off the meet or postpone competition until better weather at any point. Indoor events are less subject to cancellation. An athlete may withdraw from competition if he or she is injured or ill. However, nerves and fear are not good reasons to quit a competition. Part of climbing up the ranks is learning to cope with such feelings. Some athletes actually thrive on the nervous tension.

The expenses of a sport can also be overwhelming. In addition to specialized equipment and clothing, the athlete must pay for a coach, travel expenses, competition fees, and, depending on the sport, time at the gym. Tennis, golf, figure skating, and skiing are among the most expensive sports. And even after all the hard work, practice, and financial sacrifice, making big money is a rarity.

## Outlook

On the whole, the outlook for the field of professional sports is healthy, but the number of jobs will not increase dramatically. Some sports, however, may become more popular, which will mean greater opportunities for higher salaries, cash prizes, and commercial endorsements.

# TO LEARN MORE ABOUT ATHLETES

## Books

Coffey, Wayne. *Carl Lewis: The Triumph of Discipline.* Woodbridge, Conn.: Blackbirch Press, 1992

Freedman, Russell. *Babe Didrikson Zaharias.* New York: Clarion, 1999.

Krull, Kathleen. *Lives of the Athletes : Thrills, Spills (And What the Neighbors Thought).* New York: Harcourt Brace, 1997.

Rudeen, Kenneth. *Jackie Robinson.* New York: HarperTrophy, 1996.

Stewart, Mark. *Florence Griffith-Joyner.* Danbury, Conn.: Children's Press, 1997.

Stewart, Mark. *Tiger Woods: Driving Force.* Danbury, Conn.: Children's Press, 1998.

Updyke, Rosemary Kissinger. *Jim Thorpe, the Legend Remembered.* New York: Pelican, 1997.

## Websites
### Sports Illustrated for Kids
*http://www.sikids.com/*
An on-line magazine providing news about current athletes and sports

### United States Olympic Committee
*http://www.olympic-usa.org/*
Official site of this committee headquartered in Colorado Springs

### USA Track & Field
*http://www.usatf.org/*
A resource for information about current athletes as well as members of the hall of fame, plus current news and membership

### Women in Sports
*http://www.makeithappen.com/wis/index.html*
Provides information about and links to women in all kinds of sports

## Where to Write
Young people who are interested in becoming professional athletes should contact the professional organizations for the sport in which they would like to compete, such as the National Tennis Association, the Professional Golf Association, or the National Bowling Association. Ask for information on requirements, training centers, coaches, and so on.

**American Alliance for Health, Physical Education, Recreation, and Dance**
1900 Association Drive
Reston, VA 20191
Tel: 703/476-3400
*http://www.aahperd.org/*
For additional information on athletics

**Amateur Athletic Union**
c/o The Walt Disney World Resort
P.O. Box 10000
Lake Buena Vista, FL 32830-1000
Tel: 407/934-7200
*http://www.aausports.org/*
For a free brochure and information on the Junior Olympics and more

# HOW TO BECOME A TEACHER

## The Job

Elementary-school teachers instruct pupils from the first through sixth grades. They develop teaching outlines and lesson plans, give lectures, organize discussions and activities, keep class-attendance records, assign homework, and evaluate student progress. They usually work with one group of pupils for the entire school day, teaching several subjects and supervising lunch and recess.

Most elementary-school teachers teach one grade. In some smaller schools, however, grades are combined. And there are still a few elementary schools in remote rural areas, where all eight grades are taught by one teacher.

As an elementary-school teacher, you'll teach language, science, mathematics, and social studies. In the classroom, various methods are used to educate students. You may read to them from a book, assign group projects, and show films. You'll teach them educational games and help them come up with ways to remember new information. Students in kindergarten and the first and second grades are taught the basic skills—reading, writing, counting, and telling time. Older students are taught history, geography, math, English, and handwriting.

Creating interesting exercises and activities takes time outside of the classroom. In addition to this extra work, you'll prepare daily lesson plans, including lists of student assignments. You'll also grade papers and tests, keep a record of each student's progress, and prepare reports for parents. You'll meet with teacher aides to discuss how they can help in the classroom. You'll keep the classroom orderly and neat and decorate the desks and bulletin boards.

Music, art, and physical education are usually taught by teachers who specialize in those areas. Art teachers develop art projects, gather supplies, and help students develop drawing, painting, sculpture, mural design, ceramics, and other artistic abilities. Some art teachers also teach the history of art and organize field trips to local museums. Music teachers teach music appreciation and history. They also direct student choruses, bands, or orchestras or simply accompany a classroom of students in singing. Music teachers are often responsible for organizing school pageants, musicals, and plays. Physical-education teachers help students develop coordination, strength, and stamina as well as social skills, such as self-confidence and good sportsmanship. Physical-education teachers often coach school sports teams and organize field days and community activities.

Elementary-school children are taught social skills along with general school subjects. The teacher helps the students learn right from wrong. He or she also maintains a system of rewards and punishments.

Recent developments in school programs have led to such concepts as the ungraded or multi-age classroom, where one or more teachers work with students within a small age range. Some schools are also turning to bilingual education in which students are instructed throughout the day in two languages, either by one bilingual teacher or two teachers who concentrate on different languages.

## Requirements

*High School*   Your school's college-preparatory program will offer advanced courses in English, mathematics, science, history, and government to prepare you for an education degree. Art, music, physical education, and extracurricular activities will give you the wide knowledge necessary to teach a variety of subjects. Composition, journalism, and communications classes will help you develop good writing and speaking skills.

*Postsecondary*   About 500 teacher-education programs are offered in the United States. Most of these programs are designed to meet the requirements of the state in which they're located. Some states may require that you pass a test before being admitted to an education program. In most states, an elementary-education teacher must major in elementary education. Programs vary among colleges but may include introduction courses in the teaching of reading, guidance of the young child, children's literature, and teaching language arts. Practice teaching, also called student teaching, in an actual school situation is usually part of the program. The student is placed in a school to work with a full-time teacher. During this period, the student observes how lessons are presented and how the classroom is managed, learns how to keep records of attendance and grades, and gets actual experience in handling the class—both under supervision and alone. Some states require a master's degree; teachers with master's degrees can earn higher salaries. Private schools do not require an education degree.

**Licensing and Certification** Public-school teachers must be licensed under regulations established by the Department of Education of the state in which they are teaching. Not all states require teachers in private or parochial schools to be licensed. When you've received your teaching degree, you may request that a transcript of your college record be sent to the licensure section of the state Department of Education. If you have met all the requirements, you will receive a certificate saying you are eligible to teach in the public schools of your state. In some states, you may have to take additional tests.

**Other Requirements** The desire to teach is based on a love of children and a dedication to their welfare. You must respect children as individuals, with likes and dislikes, strengths and weaknesses of their own. You must be patient and self-disciplined and have a high standard of personal conduct. Teachers make a powerful impression on children and you'll want to be a good role model.

## Exploring

Volunteer to teach elementary classes in Sunday school or become an assistant in a scout troop. You might work as a counselor in a summer camp or assist a recreation director in a park or community center. Look for opportunities to tutor younger students or coach children's athletic teams. Your local community theater may need directors and assistants for summer children's productions. Many day-care centers hire high-school students for late-afternoon and weekend work. Working with preschoolers will give you a sense of a child's learning processes and the methods used to educate young children.

## Employers

Elementary-school teachers are needed at public and private schools, parochial schools, Montessori schools, and day-care centers that offer full-day elementary programs. Although some rural areas have elementary schools, most are in towns and cities. Teachers are also finding opportunities in charter schools—smaller, deregulated schools that receive public funding.

## Starting Out

After completing the teacher-certification process, including student teaching, your college's placement office will help you find full-time work. Also, the Departments of Education of some states provide listings of job openings. And many schools advertise teaching positions in the classified ads of major newspapers. You may also want to contact the principals and superintendents of schools in which you'd especially like to work. While waiting for full-time work, you can work as a substitute teacher. In urban areas with many schools, you may be able to substitute full-time.

## Advancement

Most teachers become experts in the job they have chosen. Usually salaries increase as teachers gain experience. Additional training or study can also bring more money.

A few teachers may advance to the position of principal. Others may work up to supervisory positions, and some may become helping teachers. These teachers help other teachers to find appropriate instructional materials and develop their courses of study. Others may go into teacher education at a college or university. Additional education is required for most of these positions. Some teachers also become guidance counselors or resource-room teachers.

## Work Environment

Usually, you'll work in a pleasant environment, although some older schools may have poor heating and electrical systems. The job of the elementary-school teacher is not strenuous, but it can be trying. You must stand for many hours each day, do a lot of talking, exhibit energy and enthusiasm, and handle any discipline problems. But problems with students are usually overshadowed by the successes. The work of an elementary teacher can be confining, because you are with your pupils constantly throughout the day's activities. School hours are generally 8:00 A.M. to 3:00 P.M., Monday through Friday. Teachers are usually able to take all school holidays, including winter and spring vacations. Many teachers take college courses during the summer months to help them do a better job. Some states require teachers to take such courses to renew or upgrade their teaching licenses.

## Earnings

Most teachers are contracted to work nine months of the year, though some contracts are made for ten or twelve months. (When children are not present, teachers are expected to do summer teaching, planning, or other school-related work.)

The National Education Association's (NEA) *Rankings of the States, 1997,* reported the average annual teacher salary was $38,611, ranging from $26,764 in South Dakota to $50,647 in Alaska. The American Federation of Teachers also released survey results for 1997–98. Its report found that the average beginning salary for a teacher with a bachelor's degree was $25,700. The average maximum salary for a teacher with a master's degree was $44,694. Teachers can supplement their earnings through teaching summer classes, coaching sports, sponsoring a club, or other extracurricular work.

Teachers have unions that bargain with schools over wages, hours, and benefits. Most teachers join the American Federation of Teachers or the National Education Association (NEA). Depending on the state, benefits include a retirement plan, sick leave, and health and life insurance. Some systems grant teachers sabbatical leave.

## Outlook

The U.S. Department of Education predicts that 1 million new teachers will be needed by the year 2008 to meet rising enrollment and replace retiring teachers. The NEA believes this will be a difficult challenge because of low teacher salaries. Higher salaries will be necessary to attract new teachers and keep experienced ones, along with other changes such as smaller classes and safer schools. Other challenges for the profession involve attracting more men. The percentage of male teachers continues to drop.

To improve education for all children, changes are being considered by some districts. Some private companies are now managing public schools. Although some believe that a private company can provide better facilities, faculty, and equipment, this has not been proved. Teacher organizations are concerned about taking school management away from communities and turning it over to corporations. Charter schools and voucher programs are two other controversial alternatives to traditional public education. Charter schools are small schools that are publicly funded but not guided by the rules and regulations of traditional public schools. They are viewed by some as places of innovation and improved educational methods, but others see charter schools as ill-equipped and unfairly funded with money that could be used to benefit local school districts. Vouchers, which exist in only a few cities, allow students to attend private schools by using public money for tuition. These vouchers are paid for with public tax dollars. In theory, the vouchers allow for more choices in education for poor and minority students, but private schools still have the option of being highly selective in their admissions.

# TO LEARN MORE ABOUT TEACHERS

## Books

Davidson, Margaret. *Helen Keller's Teacher.* New York: Scholastic, 1996.

McDaniel, Melissa. *W.E.B. Dubois: Scholar and Civil Rights Activist.* Danbury, Conn.: Franklin Watts, 1999.

Shephard, Marie Tennant. *Maria Montessori: Teacher of Teachers.* Minneapolis: Lerner, 1996.

Wilker, Josh. *Confucius: Philosopher and Teacher.* Danbury, Conn.: Franklin Watts, 1999.

## Websites

**American Federation of Teachers**
*http://www.aft.org*

**National Education Association**
*http://www.nea.org*

## Where to Write
**American Federation of Teachers**
555 New Jersey Avenue, N.W.
Washington, DC 20001
202/879-4400
For information about careers and about the current
issues affecting teachers

**National Education Association**
1201 16th Street, N.W.
Washington, DC 20036
202/833-4000
For information about careers and about the current
issues affecting teachers

# TO LEARN MORE ABOUT WILMA RUDOLPH

## Books

Biracree, Tom, and Matina S. Horner. *Wilma Rudolph.* New York: Chelsea House, 1990.

Coffey, Wayne, R. *Wilma Rudolph.* Woodbridge, Conn.: Blackbirch Press, 1997.

Kent, Deborah, and Kathryn A. Quinlan. *Extraordinary People with Disabilities.* Danbury, Conn.: Children's Press, 1996.

Krull, Kathleen, and David Diaz (illustrator). *Wilma Unlimited: How Wilma Rudolph Became the World's Fastest Woman.* San Diego: Harcourt Brace and Company, 1996.

Ruth, Amy. *Wilma Rudolph.* Minneapolis: Lerner Publishing Group, 1999.

Sherrow, Victoria, and Larry Johnson (illustrator). *Wilma Rudolph.* Minneapolis: Lerner Publishing Group, 2000.

# Websites

## It Wouldn't Have Happened Without Her

*http://www.lifetimetv.com/exclusives/20th_century/frame set.shtml/wilmarud.html*

A look at Rudolph's life and accomplishments

## The National Women's Hall of Fame

*http://www.greatwomen.org/rudlph.htm*

Rudolph's biography at the National Women's Hall of Fame website

## Tennessee State University Hall of Fame

*http://www.tnstate.edu/athletics/tsuhalfl.html#Wilma Rudolph*

Rudoph's biographical entry at her university's Hall of Fame website

## Wilma Ran and the World Went Wild

*http://www.espn.go.com/sportscentury/ features/00016444.html*

A profile of one of the twentieth-century's greatest athletes

## Women in History: Wilma Rudolph

*http://www.lkwdpl.org/wihohio/rudo-wil.htm*

A thorough online biography, plus links to other sites

## Interesting Places to Visit

**The Basketball Hall of Fame**

P.O. Box 179
1150 West Columbus Avenue
Springfield, Massachusetts 01101-0179
413/781-6500

**National Baseball Hall of Fame and Museum**

25 Main Street
P.O. Box 590
Cooperstown, New York 13326
888/425-5633

**The National Soccer Hall of Fame**

18 Stadium Circle
Oneonta, New York 13820
607/432-3351

**Pro Football Hall of Fame**

2121 George Halas Drive, N.W.
Canton, Ohio 44708
330/456-8207

**Tennessee Sports Hall of Fame**

209 Seventh Avenue North
Nashville, Tennessee 37219

**USA Track & Field Hall of Fame**

200 South Capitol Avenue
Indianapolis, Indiana 46225
317/261-0500

# INDEX

Page numbers in *italics* indicate illustrations.

Jackson, Nel, 43, *44*

Kennedy, John F., 70, *71*, 73

Millrose Games, 75
music teachers, 113

National Amateur Athletic
    Union (AAU), 35, 36, 56

Olympic Games, 7, *8*, 40–43,
    *44*, 44–50, *50*, *52*, 56, *57*,
    *58*, 59–60, *61*, *62*, 62–64,
    *64*, 66. *See also* athletes.
"Operation Champ," 83

physical education, 105,
    114–115

Robinson, Jackie, *38*, 39
Roller, Eric, 105
Rudolph, Blanche (mother), 13,
    *68*
Rudolph, Charlene (sister), *68*
Rudolph, Ed (father), 13, *68*
Rudolph, Wilma Glodean, *8*,
    *17*, *23*, *41*, *44*, *48*, *52*,
    *57*, *58*, *61*, *62*, *64*, *65*,
    *68*, *69*, *71*, *72*, *77*, *79*,
    *82*, *84*, *87*, *88*, *92*, *94*,
    *96*
    Babe Zaharias Award, 78,
        *79*
    Baptist Christian Athletes,
        80
    birth of, 11

bronze medal won by, 51,
    *52*
Burt High School basketball
    career, 25–27, 52–53
Burt High School track-and-
    field career, 29–30, 80
childhood illness of, 11–12,
    18–20, 22
Christopher Columbus
    Award, 73
Clarksville parade for,
    67–70, *69*
death of, 97–99
education of, 16, 18,
    20–21, 25, 33, 55–56,
    75, 80, *82*
gold medals won by, 7, *8*,
    *61*, 66
influence of teachers on,
    20–21
James E. Sullivan Award,
    *72*, 73
media coverage of, 66–67, 85
named to Women's Sports
    Hall of Fame, *94*
National Amateur Athletic
    Union meet, 35, 36, 56
1956 Olympic Games,
    43–51, *52*, 59–60
1960 Olympic Games, 7, *8*,
    56, *57*, *58*, 59–60, *61*,
    62–64, *65*
Olympic qualifications, 42
publicity tours, 70–73
religious beliefs of, 16
retirement of, 78

# ABOUT THE AUTHOR

Alice Flanagan lives in Chicago, Illinois, and writes books for children and teachers. Ever since she was a young girl, Ms. Flanagan has enjoyed writing. Today, she has more than seventy books published on a wide variety of topics. Some of the books she has written include biographies of U.S. Presidents and First Ladies; biographies of people working in our neighborhood; phonics books for beginning readers; informational books about birds and Native Americans; and career education in the classroom.